# Diet recommendations for TCM - Spleen - Qi deficiency + spleen does not control the blood

Please check these recommendations always with a nutrition consultant, therapist, doctor or dietician. The recipes and the list of ingredients are supporting the conventional medical therapy.
The calorie disclosures of fresh ingredients (fruit and vegetables) vary according to quality and time of harvest. The contents were checked by a dietician and a nutrition consultant for the Traditional Chinese Medicine (TCM).

Author:
©2019 Josef Miligui
www.ebns.at

AF205181

Source:
The lists are created from the EBNS database for nutritional counseling. The database is used by dietitians, therapists and doctors for advising the patient / client.

Literature:
The specialist literature and the training documents of the German and Austrian dietary and traditional Chinese medicine serve as a knowledge base. We have used the documents as a basis of knowledge, adapted it to our experience and completed them.
http://di-book.com

Production and publishing:
BoD – Books on Demand, Norderstedt
ISBN: 9783746097428

**Diet recommendations for TCM - Spleen - Qi deficiency + spleen does not control the blood**

# 1 Treatment strategy

Tonify and strengthen spleen and blood-nutrient foods, kidney qi support, slightly astringent.

# 2 Avoid

n.a.

# 3 Breakfast

|  | kkal. per serving |
| --- | --- |
| Bean paste piquant sweet | 311 |
| Carrot and rice gruel soup | 101 |
| Carrot Risotto | 308 |
| Chickpeas with Raisins | 429 |
| Kuzu soup in the morning | 12 |
| Leek soup with almondmash | 115 |
| Quick flakes with compote or jam | 189 |
| Quinoa with peach | 247 |

# 4  Snack

n.a.

# 5  Lunch

# 6   Afternoon

n.a.

# 7   Dinner

# 8   Any time

# 9   Recipes

(rec.) = You can use more.
(little) = You should use less than specified
(omit) = omit.

## 9.1   8 treasures of rice

Strengthens kidney and bladder, builds up Qi, strengthens the spleen, repels moisture, reduces internal heat, prevents cancer, builds heart, calms nerves.
Cooking time approx. 1 hour
Calories p. portion: 223
4 portions

**Quantity of ingredients:**
Lily bulbs 1 table spoon / 5g. () - cool - sweet, bitter .......................................... *
Longane 1 table spoon / 5g. (yes) - warm - sweet ........................................... *
King Solomon's-seal 1 table spoon / 5g. () - neutral - sweet, bitter ................. *
Yam root, yam root tuber 1 table spoon / 5g. () - neutral - sweet .................... *
Coix (seeds) YiYi Ren 1 table spoon / 5g. (little) - cool - sweet, neutral.......... *
Rice wild (nature rice) 1 1/2 cups / 240g. (yes) - neutral - sweet, bitter..... metal
Water 8-10 cups / 800g. (yes) - cool - salty...............................................earth

**Cooking instructions:**
Each one 1 tbsp: Bai He, Longan, Yu Zhu, Da Zao, Shan Yao, Lian Mi, Yi Yi Ren, Qian Shi
Add hot water and soak for about 30 minutes. Then add 1 - 2 cups of rice (normal) and simmer for 1/2 to 1 hour until the rice is very soft. Or: Cook for about 3 hours with the herbs a congee. Then the herbs do not have to be soaked.

## 9.2   Basic recipe for a chicken broth worming

Strengthens Qi and blood, is very warm.
Cooking time approx. 2-3 hours
Calories p. portion: 90
9 portions
Allergens: L

**Quantity of ingredients:**
Chicken meat 1/2 piece / 600g. (rec.) - warm - sweet .............................. wood
Carrot 2 pieces / 150g. (rec.) - neutral - sweet...........................................earth
Leek 1 stick / 45g. (yes) - warm - acrid ................................................. metal
Celery root 1 piece / 500g. (rec.) - cool - sweet..........................................earth

Ginger fresh 2 slices / 2g. (rec.) - warm - acrid ......................................... metal
Juniper berry 1 teaspoon / 3g. (rec.) - warm - sweet, acrid, bitter ................ fire
Bay leaf 3 pieces / 2g. () - warm - acrid ..................................................... metal
Water 4 cup / 900g. (yes) - cool - salty ....................................................... earth

**Cooking instructions:**
Remove chicken parts from fat. Place chicken pieces in a saucepan with hot water and heat till it boils briefly, skimming any resulting foam. Add coarsely chopped vegetables and all spices and cook over medium heat for 2 to 3 hours. Strain the finished soup. Throw away vegetables and bones.
Tip: If you want to use the meat as a soup insert, take out after 45 minutes and return only the bones in the soup.
Refrigerate for later use.

## 9.3  Basic recipe for a reissue soup (Congee)

Warms the stomach and spleen, harmonizes the intestine, forces Qi, reduces moisture.
Cooking time approx. 2-4 hours
Calories p. portion: 140
3 portions

**Quantity of ingredients:**
Rice variety any 1 cup / 120g. (rec.) - warm - sweet ................................ metal
Water 6 cups / 700g. (yes) - cool - salty ..................................................... earth

**Cooking instructions:**
Cook rice and water in a ratio of about 1: 6. The amount of water determines the thickness of the mash (matter of taste).
Put the rice in a saucepan with a heavy lid. It is important to simmer the rice after a short boil on the slightest flame, otherwise it burns.
Boil the rice for 2-4 hours. The longer it cooks, the more it strengthens. If you want to eat the dish for breakfast, you can put the rice on just before bedtime.
To be on the safe side, you should first check the behavior of your pot and cooker under observation for a similar amount of time, so that nothing burns.
Refrigerate for later use.

## 9.4   Basic recipe for a vegetable soup, nutritious

Strengthens spleen and lung, regulates Qi flow, builds up Qi, dries out, passes downwardly, strengthens stomach Qi.
Cooking time approx. 2-3 hours
Calories p. portion: 48
5 portions
Allergens: L

**Quantity of ingredients:**
Olive oil 1 table spoon / 4g. (little) - cool - sweet ..........................................earth
Onion white 1 piece / 60g. (yes) - warm - acrid ......................................... metal
Carrot 3 pieces / 200g. (rec.) - neutral - sweet .............................................earth
Parsnip 3/8 lbs - 6oz / 150g. (rec.) - cool - bitter ...........................................fire
Celery root 1 cup / 100g. (rec.) - cool - sweet .............................................earth
Ginger fresh 1/2 teaspoon / 2g. (rec.) - warm - acrid................................. metal
Lemon 1/2 piece / 25g. (omit) - cold - sour................................................. wood
Juniper berry 6 pieces / 6g. (rec.) - warm - sweet, acrid, bitter.....................fire
Thyme dried 1 pinch / 1g. () - warm - bitter ............................................... metal
Lovage 1 table spoon / 3g. (rec.) - warm - acrid, bitter.............................. metal
Bay leaf 2 leaves / 1g. () - warm - acrid...................................................... metal
Salt 1 pinch / 1g. (little) - cold - salty ........................................................ water
Water 3 cups / 650g. (yes) - cool - salty ......................................................earth

**Cooking instructions:**
Cut the vegetables into cubes.
Heat oil in hot pot, fry shortly onions and vegetables.
Add cold water, then add ginger, bay leaf and lemon juice.
Season with juniper, thyme and lovage. Cover for 2 - 3 hours on a low heat and simmer.
The used vegetables should be thrown away.
The basic recipe serves as a soup base and to refine vegetables, legumes or cereals.
If you want to eat vegetable soup immediately, add the desired vegetables half an hour before.
Refrigerate for later use.

## 9.5  Bean paste piquant sweet

Strengthens spleen, stomach and kidney, strengthens middle as well as kidneys Jang, Yin and Jing.
Cooking time approx. 1 hour
Calories p. portion: 311
1 portion
Allergens: MO

**Quantity of ingredients:**
Black beans 1 cup / 120g. (little) - neutral - sweet....................................water
Ginger fresh 1 inch / 3g. (rec.) - warm - acrid............................................metal
Boxhorn clover seeds 1/2 teaspoon / 2g. (rec.) - warm - bitter........................ *
Tomato paste 1 table spoon / 10g. () - cold - sweet-sour .........................wood
Olive oil 2 table spoons / 20g. (little) - cool - sweet ..................................earth
Pumpkin seed oil 1 dash / 3g. (little) - warm - sweet.................................earth
Horseradish 1 teaspoon (grated) / 2g. (yes) - neutral - sweet, little acrid ..metal
Pepper (ground) 1 pinch / 0,5g. () - warm - acrid ......................................metal
Garlic 2 cloves / 3g. (little) - hot - acrid......................................................metal
Salt 1 pinch / 1g. (little) - cold - salty .......................................................water
Sugar molasses 2 table spoons / 20g. (yes) - cold - sweet........................earth
Lemon peel 1/2 piece / 1g. (rec.) - cool - bitter..............................................fire
Water 1 1/2 cups / 50g. (yes) - cool - salty.................................................earth

**Cooking instructions:**
Boil beans (with spices and ginger), drain water and puree. Season with spices. Refine with sugar beet syrup and lemon peel.

## 9.6  Beef soup with carrots, leeks, bay leaves

Strengthens spleen Qi, strengthens blood and Qi, moisturizes, relaxes, builds up Qi, spreads, strengthens spleen and liver, regulates Qi flow, strengthens stomach Qi.
Cooking time approx. 2-3 hours
Calories p. portion: 194
5 portions

**Quantity of ingredients:**
Beef meat 1 lbs / 500g. (rec.) - warm - sweet.............................................earth
Carrot 2 pieces / 200g. (rec.) - neutral - sweet ...........................................earth
Leek 1/2 piece / 150g. (yes) - warm - acrid .................................................metal
Bay leaf 3 leaves / 1g. () - warm - acrid......................................................metal
Corn Grease (Polenta) 1 table spoon / 10g. (rec.) - neutral - sweet...........earth
Water 2 cup / 450g. (yes) - cool - salty.......................................................earth
Salt 1 pinch / 0,5g. (little) - cold - salty ......................................................water

**Cooking instructions:**
In a saucepan with water (enough to cover the meat), add beef soup meat or leg slice and simmer for a moment; then pour off the broth, rinse the meat with hot water (this will save you from foaming), clean the pot and put the meat in hot water again; add chopped carrot, leek, corn and bay leaf; simmer until the meat is cooked.

## 9.7  Beluga lentil stew with vegetables

Tonifies Qi and blood, forces kidneys and spleen, dissipates heat and moisture.
Cooking time approx. 20 min
Calories p. portion: 201
5 portions

**Quantity of ingredients:**
Lentils 1 1/2 cups / 240g. (little) - neutral - sweet, sour ............................ water
Water 4-5 cups / 500g. (yes) - cool - salty.................................................earth
Carrot 3 pieces / 150g. (rec.) - neutral - sweet ..........................................earth
Leek 1 piece / 300g. (yes) - warm - acrid ................................................. metal
Kohlrabi 1/2 piece / 200g. (rec.) - neutral - acrid, sweet............................earth
Tomato 2 pieces / 80g. (omit) - cold - sweet-sour .................................... wood
Onion white 1 piece / 50g. (yes) - warm - acrid ......................................... metal
Bay leaf 2 leaves / 1g. () - warm - acrid...................................................... metal
Fennel 1 piece / 250g. (rec.) - warm - sweet, little acrid............................earth
Star anise 2 pieces / 1g. (rec.) - hot - acrid ............................................. metal
Juniper berry 6 pieces / 2g. (rec.) - warm - sweet, acrid, bitter.....................fire
Chili (pod or ground) 1 pinch / 0,2g. (rec.) - hot - acrid............................. metal
Olive oil 3 table spoons / 30g. (little) - cool - sweet ..................................earth
Salt 1 pinch / 1g. (little) - cold - salty ...................................................... water
Ginger fresh 1/2 teaspoon / 2g. (rec.) - warm - acrid................................ metal
Black caraway 1 pinch / 1g. (rec.) - warm - acrid, sweet ................................. *

**Cooking instructions:**
Heat oil in hot pot. Fry onions and add diced vegetables and spices, lentils (washed well) and salt. Cover with cold water (3 fingers wide) and cook for 20 minutes on a low heat.
Sprinkle with fresh herbs and black cumin.

Goes well with rice!

## 9.8 Black-eyed beans stew

Strengthens spleen and kidney, is very nutritious, warms the stomach and spleen, harmonizes the intestine, forces Qi, strengthens stomach and kidney, strengthens spleen and kidney.
Cooking time approx. 20 min
Calories p. portion: 140
5 portions

### Quantity of ingredients:
Black-eyed peas 1 cup / 100g. (little) - neutral - sweet, acrid ................... water
Rice variety any 1 1/2 cups / 200g. (rec.) - warm - sweet .......................... metal
Water 10 cups / 1000g. (yes) - cool - salty ................................................. earth

### Cooking instructions:
Soak the beans overnight and strain.

In a ratio of 1: 2, simmer the beans together with the rice in the Water. Depending on how hot the flame is and how thin the dish should be, more water must be added.

Variation: Add vegetables fried in oil, such as carrots, celery tubers, onions or leeks.

## 9.9 Boiled fillet with potatoebiscuits (Austrian classic Tafelspitz)

Strengthens spleen Qi, strengthens blood and Qi, moisturizes, relaxes, builds up Qi, spreads, forces Qi, forces spleen, relieves inflammation, moisturizes.
Cooking time approx. 3 hours
Calories p. portion: 454
8 portions
Allergens: L

### Quantity of ingredients:
Onion white 1 piece / 50g. (yes) - warm - acrid ......................................... metal
Corn germ oil 1 table spoon / 10g. () - neutral - sweet ............................... earth
Water 32 cup - 1 gallon / 0g. (yes) - cool - salty ....................................... earth
Beef meat 5,4 lbs - 70oz cap of rump / 1800g. (rec.) - warm - sweet ......... earth
Beef meatbones 4n slices with bone marrow / 0g. (yes) - warm - sweet .... earth
Salt 1 pinch / 0,5g. (little) - cold - salty ..................................................... water
Peppercorns 15 pieces / 0g. (rec.) - warm - acrid .................................... metal
Parsnip 1 piece / 0g. (rec.) - cool - bitter ...................................................... fire
Carrot 2 pieces / 0g. (rec.) - neutral - sweet .............................................. earth

Celery root 1 slice / 0g. (rec.) - cool - sweet..............................................earth
Parsley root 2 pieces / 0g. (rec.) - cool - sweet .......................................earth
Leek 1/2 stick / 0g. (yes) - warm - acrid........................................ metal
Chives 1 table spoon (chopped) / 7g. (rec.) - warm - acrid...................... metal
Potato 2,2 lbs / 1000g. (yes) - neutral - sweet...........................................earth
Sunflower oil 2 table spoons / 20g. (little) - cool - sweet ...........................earth
Salt 1 pinch / 0,5g. (little) - cold - salty ...................................................... water

## Cooking instructions:

Halve the onions, but do not peel. Brown onions in a pan with fat on the cut surfaces very dark. Wash meat and bones briefly with warm water, drain.

Heat the water till it boils, put in meat and cook gently. Always scoop up rising foam. As soon as no more foam rises, add peppercorns and the onion. Clean and cut root and leeks and add after about two and a half hours cooking time. Simmer for another half hour.

Remove boiled beef from the soup, pour through a sieve and season with salt. Cut roots into bite-sized pieces. Add the soup together with the marrow bones and leave it under the boiling point. Cut the boiled beef into finger-thick slices against the grain, place in the soup, heat again, sprinkle with a little chives.

In addition, cook and peel the potatoes in salted water. Stomp roughly or cut finely. Fry in a pan with the oil crispy.

# 9.10 Carp soup

Nourishing and slightly warming, strengthens the middle and the lower heater, removes moisture.
Cooking time approx. 2 hours
Calories p. portion: 166
6 portions
Allergens: DO

## Quantity of ingredients:

Carp 1,1 lbs / 500g. (rec.) - neutral - salty..................................................water
Salt 1 pinch / 1g. (little) - cold - salty ...................................................... water
Vinegar (Apple vinegar) 1 teaspoon / 3g. (little) - warm - sour, bitter ........ wood
Thyme 1 Twig / 3g. (rec.) - warm - bitter ......................................................... *
Juniper berry 8 pieces / 3g. (rec.) - warm - sweet, acrid, bitter.....................fire
Carrot 2 pieces / 200g. (rec.) - neutral - sweet ...............................................earth
Leek 1 piece / 200g. (yes) - warm - acrid................................................metal
Onion white 1 piece / 60g. (yes) - warm - acrid..........................................metal
Ginger fresh 1/2 teaspoon / 2g. (rec.) - warm - acrid................................metal
Bay leaf 3 leaves / 1g. () - warm - acrid................................................metal
White wine 1/2 cup / 125g. (yes) - cool - sweet, bitter, acrid ....................wood

Basil 3 leaves / 1g. (rec.) - warm - acrid, bitter ............................................... fire
Water 4 cup / 800g. (yes) - cool - salty ....................................................... earth

**Cooking instructions:**
Preparation: When shopping at the fishmonger, remove the fillets from a medium-sized, whole carp and also pack the fish head, spine with bones and tail.

Cut the fillets into 1 cm cubes; salt and set aside.

Place fish head, backbone and tail of carp in plenty of cold water; heat till it boils and scoop the foam; add a dash of vinegar, a fresh sprig of thyme, juniper berries; Add carrot, a piece of leek and chopped onion; add a thick slice of ginger, some peppercorns, 1 bay leaf, salt; simmer for about 1 1/2 hours and pour the stock through a sieve.

Put the carp pieces in a saucepan; pour a shot of white wine; Add rose paprika, basil leaves, finely ground carrots, dried thyme and the stock and warm; Boil the ingredients for about 5 minutes until the fish pieces are cooked.
Variants: Thicken the soup with kuzu or mashed potatoes.
This fits: baguette and dry white wine.

## 9.11 Carrot and rice gruel soup

Warms the stomach and spleen, harmonizes the intestine, forces Qi, reduces moisture, strengthens spleen and liver, regulates Qi flow, moisturizes, relaxes, builds up Qi, spreads.
Cooking time approx. 10 min
Calories p. portion: 101
1 portion

**Quantity of ingredients:**
Basic recipe for a rice soup (Congee) 1 cup / 120g. (rec.) - neutral - sweet..... *
Carrot 2 pieces / 100g. (rec.) - neutral - sweet ........................................... earth
Salt 1 teaspoon / 4g. (little) - cold - salty .................................................... water

**Cooking instructions:**
Peel and grate carrots. Heat the rice soup (according to the basic recipe) till it boils and add the grated carrots and salt. Cook for 10 minutes.

## 9.12 Carrot Risotto

Forces stomach, spleen and liver, regulates Qi flow, relaxes, builds up Qi, spreads, dries out, passes downwardly, strengthens stomach Qi, nourishes blood and liver, harmonizes liver and spleen, forces eyesight, preserves the fluids, contracts.
Cooking time approx. 45 min
Calories p. portion: 308
2 portions
Allergens: GL

**Quantity of ingredients:**
Olive oil 1/2 teaspoon / 5g. (little) - cool - sweet..........................................earth
Onion (spring onion) 2 table spoons / 7g. (yes) - warm - acrid.................. metal
Nutmeg 1 pinch / 0,3g. (rec.) - warm - acrid............................................... metal
Parsley 1/2 bunch / 25g. (rec.) - warm - bitter............................................ wood
Rice variety any 10 cups / 100g. (rec.) - warm - sweet ............................. metal
Rice variety any 1/4 lbs - 4oz / 100g. (rec.) - warm - sweet...................... metal
Carrot 5/8 lbs - 8oz / 250g. (rec.) - neutral - sweet....................................earth
Basic recipe for a vegetable soup (nutritious) 1 cup / 280g. (rec.) - neutral - *. *
Basil (fresh) 1/2 teaspoon / 2g. (rec.) - warm - acrid, bitter ...................... metal
Salt 1 pinch / 1g. (little) - cold - salty ........................................................ water
Pepper (ground) 1 pinch / 0,3g. () - warm - acrid ...................................... metal

**Cooking instructions:**
Heat the oil in a pan, fry the onions in a glassy and very soft manner. Add parsley, sauté briefly. Add rice, carrots and nutmeg, sauté briefly while stirring. Add the vegetable stock, season with fennel and basil, heat till it boils and cook for about 20 minutes until the rice and carrots are well. Stir from time to time and add some vegetable stock if necessary. The risotto should be slightly soupy. Just before the end of the cooking time mix in the white wine and simmer the risotto for a short while. Remove risotto from the heat, mix in Parmesan.

## 9.13 Chicken in an Italian style

Forces Qi, blood and Jing, middle heater, builds up spleen and stomach, nourishes Qi, forces essence, preserves the fluids, moisturizes.
Cooking time approx. 1 hour
Calories p. portion: 410
4 portions
Allergens: M

## Quantity of ingredients:

Olive oil 3 table spoons / 30g. (little) - cool - sweet ....................................earth
Chicken meat 1 piece (cut into 8 pieces) / 700g. (rec.) - warm - sweet..... wood
Garlic 3 cloves / 5g. (little) - hot - acrid.....................................................metal
Rosemary 1/2 teaspoon / 2g. (rec.) - warm - bitter........................................fire
Salt 1 pinch / 1g. (little) - cold - salty ........................................................water
Pepper (ground) 1 pinch / 0,5g. () - warm - acrid .....................................metal
Water 1 cup / 20g. (yes) - cool - salty.........................................................earth
Rice Basmati 1 cup / 120g. (yes) - neutral - sweet.....................................metal
Water 6 cups / 400g. (yes) - cool - salty......................................................earth
Salt 1 pinch / 1g. (little) - cold - salty ........................................................water
Lettuce 1 piece / 300g. (little) - cool - sweet, bitter.........................................fire
Olive oil 2 table spoons / 20g. (little) - cool - sweet ...................................earth
Lemon juice 1/4 piece / 7g. (rec.) - cold - sour ......................................... wood
Salt 1 pinch / 1g. (little) - cold - salty ........................................................water
Honey 1 pinch / 2g. (little) - cold - sweet ...................................................earth


## Cooking instructions:

In a heavy pan (with lid) heat 1 tbsp of olive oil at low temperature. Add the chicken pieces and fry for a few minutes. Once they start to take on color, add the remaining 2 tablespoons of olive oil and garlic. Turn the chicken parts in the oil and sprinkle with rosemary, salt and pepper. Pour with a little water and heat till it boils. Reduce the heat, put on the lid and stew the chicken for 35 to 45 minutes.

In between, check again and again whether there is enough cooking water, and if necessary, add 1 to 2 tablespoons of water each time.

As soon as the meat comes off the bone, spread the chicken parts on the plates, deglaze the roast residue in the braised pan with a few tablespoons of water or wine and spread over the meat as a sauce.

In the meantime, cook the rice in a saucepan with (1:6) salted water, on a low heat.

Wash and spin the lettuce, finely chop and serve in a bowl. In a small bowl, mix the olive oil, lemon juice, mustard, salt and honey well and add to the salad and add it to the salad.

## 9.14 Chicken soup with angelica root and buckthorn fruit

Strengthens spleen and nourishes the blood and Yin of the liver, forces Qi and blood, is very warming.
Cooking time approx. 1 1/2 hours
Calories p. portion: 77
3 portions
Allergens: LO

### Quantity of ingredients:
Basic recipe for a chicken soup (warming) 2 cup / 500g. (rec.) - warm - * ....... *
Bocksdorn fruits (goji berry dried 1/8 lbs - 2oz / 50g. () - cool - ............... wood

### Cooking instructions:
When you cook chicken broth according to basic recipes add angelica root and willowberry fruits in the last 40 minutes.

Ingestion: Drink 2-3 cups of broth daily.


## 9.15 Chickpeas with Raisins

Strengthens spleen and liver, regulates Qi flow, moisturizes, relaxes, builds up Qi, spreads, strengthens spleen and heart, softens, passes downwardly, warms the stomach and spleen, harmonizes the intestine, forces Qi, reduces moisture.
Cooking time approx. 45 min
Calories p. portion: 429
2 portions
Allergens: EGO

### Quantity of ingredients:
Chickpeas 1 cup / 120g. (little) - cool - sweet, salty ................................... water
Hijiki 1 table spoon / 7g. () - cold - salty.................................................... water
Salt 1 pinch / 0,5g. (little) - cold - salty ..................................................... water
Sunflower oil 1 table spoon / 10g. (little) - cool - sweet ............................. earth
Carrot 2 pieces / 160g. (rec.) - neutral - sweet........................................... earth
Raisins 2 table spoons / 18g. (rec.) - warm - sweet ................................... earth
Ginger fresh 1/2 teaspoon / 2g. (rec.) - warm - acrid.................................. metal
Cumin (Caraway seed) 1 pinch / 0,2g. (rec.) - warm - acrid ...................... metal
Lemon juice 1 dash / 1g. (rec.) - cold - sour................................................ wood
Sour cream 15% fat 1 table spoon / 8g. (omit) - cool - sour ...................... wood
Turmeric (yellow root) 1 pinch / 0,2g. (yes) - warm - bitter ............................. *

Soybean milk 1 dash / 1g. (yes) - cool - sweet............................................earth
Coriander 1 pinch / 0,2g. (rec.) - warm - acrid...........................................metal
Soy sauce 1 dash / 1g. (little) - cold - salty.................................................water
Rice round grain 1/2 cup / 60g. (rec.) - neutral - sweet ...........................metal
Water 3 cups / 250g. (yes) - cool - salty.....................................................earth
Salt 1 pinch / 1g. (little) - cold - salty .......................................................water

## Cooking instructions:
Preparation:
Soak chickpeas in cold water for several hours or overnight.

After that:
Pour soaking water away; put the chickpeas in cold water; Add 1 tbsp
Hijiki and cook the chickpeas bite-proof; Add salt at the end of the
cooking time.

Separately:
In a hot pan, fry oil, chopped carrots (more than chickpeas), raisins,
grated ginger, plenty of cumin and salt until the
carrots are half cooked; add the chickpeas and sea algae; Add lemon
juice, a little sour cream, turmeric, soy or rice milk; a pinch of cilantro,
add some soy sauce; Let it soak for a few minutes over low heat until
the carrots are cooked.
Put the round grain rice with the water, salt and cook for about 20
minutes.

# 9.16 Clear soup from goose

Forces spleen, stomach and lungs, relieves weakness, forces Qi, calms
the stomach, gets Qi moving, directs upwards, strengthens spleen and
liver, regulates Qi flow, moisturizes, relaxes, builds up Qi, spreads.
Cooking time approx. 2-3 hours
Calories p. portion: 334
6 portions
Allergens:
## Quantity of ingredients:
Goose parts 1,1 lbs / 500g. (yes) - neutral - sweet...................................metal
Carrot 1 piece / 100g. (rec.) - neutral - sweet...........................................earth
Onion (shallot) 1 piece / 25g. (yes) - warm - acrid, sweet ........................metal
Leek 1 piece / 250g. (yes) - warm - acrid .................................................metal
Parsley 1 Twig / 4g. (rec.) - warm - bitter .................................................wood
Lovage 1 Twig / 4g. (rec.) - warm - acrid, bitter.........................................metal
Water 4 cup / 1000g. (yes) - cool - salty.....................................................earth
Salt 1 pinch / 0,5g. (little) - cold - salty .....................................................water

**Cooking instructions:**
Simmer goose pieces with vegetables and herbs for 2-3 hours. Sift through a fine cloth and cool. Degrease and store in the refrigerator.

## 9.17 Indian Dal soup

Reduces internal heat and moisture, softens, passes downwardly, strengthens spleen and liver, regulates Qi flow, moisturizes, relaxes, builds up Qi, spreads, forces liver and kidney, reduces damp heat.
Cooking time approx. 30 min
Calories p. portion: 256
2 portions
Allergens: EN

**Quantity of ingredients:**
Lentils 3/8 lbs - 6oz / 175g. (little) - neutral - sweet, sour .......................... water
Sesame oil 3 table spoons / 30g. (little) - cool - sweet ............................... earth
Carrot 1 piece / 100g. (rec.) - neutral - sweet................................................ earth
Onion (shallot) 1 piece / 15g. (yes) - warm - acrid, sweet ........................ metal
Water 1 1/2 cups / 200g. (yes) - cool - salty................................................ earth
Ginger fresh 2 slices / 1g. (rec.) - warm - acrid .......................................... metal
Salt 1 pinch / 0,5g. (little) - cold - salty ...................................................... water
Soy sauce 1 teaspoon / 3g. (little) - cold - salty......................................... water
Parsley 1 teaspoon (chopped) / 3g. (rec.) - warm - bitter .......................... wood
Thyme 1 teaspoon / 3g. (rec.) - warm - bitter ................................................... *
Basil 1 table spoon / 5g. (rec.) - warm - acrid, bitter...................................... fire

**Cooking instructions:**
Soak the lentils overnight.
in a hot pot, carrot, onion and a little ginger fry, pour water. Add the lentils and cook until soft. Add salt or soy sauce and cook for another 10 minutes.
Stir in parsley before serving; Sprinkle thyme or basil over it.
Variant: Other herbs such as sage, rosemary or lovage allow a variety of flavors.

## 9.18 Kidney bean pot with lamb and sage

Nourishes Yin from heart and kidney, strengthens spleen and kidney Yang, forces Qi, heats middle and lower heater, dissolves stagnation, directs upwards, moisturizes, relaxes, builds up Qi, spreads.
Cooking time approx. 1 1/2 hours
Calories p. portion: 391
4 portions
Allergens: F

**Quantity of ingredients:**

Soybean oil 3 table spoons / 30g. (little) - warm - sweet ...........................earth
Onion white 2 pieces / 120g. (yes) - warm - acrid ....................................metal
Lamb meat 5/8 oz / 200g. (yes) - warm - sweet ..........................................fire
Salt 1 pinch / 0,5g. (little) - cold - salty ....................................................water
Sage 4-5 leaves / 2g. (little) - cool - bitter, spicy...................................fire
Rosemary 1/2 teaspoon / 2g. (rec.) - warm - bitter.......................................fire
Thyme 1/2 teaspoon / 2g. (rec.) - warm - bitter ................................................. *
Kidney beans (red) 5/8 lbs - 8oz / 250g. (little) - neutral - sweet ..............water
Water 3 cups / 750g. (yes) - cool - salty ....................................................earth

**Cooking instructions:**

Soak kidney beans in water overnight and strain.
In a saucepan with oil, roast the onion. Dice the lamb and place in the pot. Season with salt, sage, rosemary and thyme.
Roast lamb well and cover pot. Cook over low heat and add ten-quarters of a gallon (750ml.) of cold water after 10 minutes.
Salt again.
Heat till it boils. Add beans to it.
Simmer for at least 1 hour until the beans and meat are tender.

# 9.19 Kuzu soup in the morning

Moisturizes, relaxes, builds up Qi, spreads, forces stomach, harmonizes middle, reduces internal heat, detoxifies, softens, passes downwardly.
Cooking time approx. 5 min
Calories p. portion: 12
1 portion
Allergens: E

**Quantity of ingredients:**

Water 1 cup / 250g. (yes) - cool - salty ...........................................earth
Soy sauce 1 dash / 2g. (little) - cold - salty....................................water
Umeboshi paste 1 knife tip / 2g. () - warm - sour ..........................water

**Cooking instructions:**

Mix kuzu with cold water and heat till it boils while stirring. Once it is glassy, remove from heat and let cool. Season with Tamari and Umeboshipaste or crushed umeboshi plums
There is always the possibility to support your stomach and intestines with this recipe, taken before the right breakfast.
A morning cure for stomach and mucous membranes. Fix the base balance.

## 9.20 Leek soup with almondmash

Gets Qi moving, moisten the lungs and large intestine, cools heat, preserves the fluids, contracts, forces Qi, forces spleen, relieves inflammation, moisturizes, relaxes, spreads.
Cooking time approx. 20 min
Calories p. portion: 115
4 portions
Allergens: HN

**Quantity of ingredients:**
Water 2 cup / 480g. (yes) - cool - salty......................................................earth
Sugar cane sugar 1 pinch / 0,3g. (little) - cool - sweet ...............................earth
Leek 2 pieces / 400g. (yes) - warm - acrid .................................................metal
Salt 1 pinch / 0,5g. (little) - cold - salty .....................................................water
Lemon juice 1/2 piece / 15g. (rec.) - cold - sour ........................................wood
Rosemary 1 Twig / 3g. (rec.) - warm - bitter...............................................fire
Pepper powder (hot) Alternative to rosemary / 0g. () - warm - bitter .............fire
Potato flour 1 table spoon / 8g. () - neutral - sweet ....................................earth
Almond puree 2 table spoons / 20g. (yes) - neutral - sweet .......................earth
Sesame oil few drops / 1g. (little) - cool - sweet ........................................earth
Pepper white (ground) 1 pinch / 0,2g. (rec.) - warm - acrid .......................metal

**Cooking instructions:**
Add a pinch of sugar to hot water, add chopped leeks and a pinch of salt; simmer until the leek is half cooked; season with lemon juice, fresh rosemary or rose paprika.
Dissolve potato flour separately in cold water; thicken the soup with it.
Add almond purée, a few drops of toasted sesame oil, pepper and simmer until the leek is cooked.
Variant (TCM):
Add mushrooms; they build up juices and soften the yangling effect of the leeks.

## 9.21 Lentils and rice stew

Strengthens spleen and liver, regulates Qi flow, moisturizes, relaxes, builds up Qi, spreads, warms the stomach
and spleen, harmonizes the intestine, forces Qi, reduces moisture, brings the liver Qi in motion, cools heat.
Cooking time approx. 25 min
Calories p. portion: 232
3 portions
Allergens: LNO

**Quantity of ingredients:**
Lentils 10 cups / 100g. (little) - neutral - sweet, sour .................................. water
Water 5 cups / 500g. (yes) - cool - salty ...................................................... earth
Rice variety any 1 cup / 120g. (rec.) - warm - sweet ................................. metal
Sesame oil 1 table spoon / 10g. (little) - cool - sweet ............................... earth
Carrot 2 pieces / 150g. (rec.) - neutral - sweet ........................................... earth
Celery sticks 2 rods / 20g. (little) - cool - sweet ......................................... earth
Cumin (Caraway seed) 1 pinch / 0,2g. (rec.) - warm - acrid ..................... metal
Salt 1 pinch / 0,5g. (little) - cold - salty ...................................................... water
Vinegar (Apple vinegar) 1 dash / 2g. (little) - warm - sour, bitter ............... wood
Parsley 2 table spoons / 18g. (rec.) - warm - bitter .................................... wood

**Cooking instructions:**
Soak the dry lentils the day before.
Heat sesame oil in a hot pot; cut carrot and celery into small pieces and
sauté; add rice, a pinch of cumin and lentils and heat till it boils.
If the lenses are soft, add salt; season with a little vinegar and garnish
with parsley.

Variant: In summer you can omit the cumin and add fresh green peas,
Chinese cabbage or celery.


# 9.22 Quick flakes with compote or jam

Forces Qi, dries out, passes downwardly, strengthens middle heater,
moisturizes, relaxes, builds up Qi, spreads, strengthens kidney Qi,
essence and brain, forces kidney, warms the middle.
Cooking time approx. 5 min
Calories p. portion: 189
2 portions
Allergens: H

**Quantity of ingredients:**
Quinoa 5-7 table spoons / 50g. (yes) - neutral - sweet, sour ......................... fire
Water 1 cup / 250g. (yes) - cool - salty ...................................................... earth
Walnuts 1 table spoon (grated) / 8g. (rec.) - warm - sweet ......................... earth
Olive oil 1 table spoon / 10g. (little) - cool - sweet ..................................... earth
Honey 2 table spoons / 20g. (little) - cold - sweet ....................................... earth
Vanilla 1 pinch / 0,2g. (rec.) - neutral - sweet ................................................... *
Anise (Common Fennel) 1 pinch / 0,2g. (rec.) - warm - acrid ..................... earth
Cardamom 1 pinch / 0,2g. () - warm - acrid ................................................ metal
Chili (pod or ground) 1 pinch / 0,1g. (rec.) - hot - acrid .............................. metal

**Cooking instructions:**
Put the quinoa flakes in a pan and add water. Boil for 3-5 minutes, pull from the fire, add nuts and compote. Add a dash of oil. Sweeten as needed with honey, whole cane sugar or agave syrup.

Spices and aromas: vanilla, anise, fennel or coriander, cardamom, a little chili.

Winter: apple compote, pear compote, fruit jam.
Summer: plum compote, apricot compote.


## 9.23 Quinoa with peach

Strengthens blood and fluids, brings blood into motion, builds up Qi, spreads, forces Qi, dries out, passes downwardly, strengthens middle heater, moisturizes.
Cooking time approx. 20 min
Calories p. portion: 248
2 portions

**Quantity of ingredients:**
Quinoa 1 cup / 100g. (yes) - neutral - sweet, sour .......................................fire
Water 1 1/2 cups / 240g. (yes) - cool - salty.................................................earth
Honey 2 teaspoons / 4g. (little) - cold - sweet ..............................................earth
Peaches 2 pieces / 240g. (yes) - warm - sour, sweet................................earth
Linseed oil 2 teaspoons / 4g. (little) - neutral - sweet ................................earth
Lemon Balm (fresh) 1 teaspoon (chopped) / 1g. () - cool - sour................ metal
Chili (pod or ground) 1 pinch / 0,1g. (rec.) - hot - acrid.............................. metal
Cinnamon ground 1 pinch / 0,2g. (rec.) - hot - acrid, sweet............................ *
Vanilla 1 pinch / 0,2g. (rec.) - neutral - sweet.................................................. *

**Cooking instructions:**
In the evening: Put quinoa in hot water and boil soft, covered 15 to 20 minutes.
In the morning: Warm up quinoa with 1 tablespoon water.
Steam lightly Peaches in a saucepan or add them fresh. Decorate with fresh lemon balm.

Summer: nectarines, apricots
Winter: Pickled fruit, pear, apples

## 9.24 Rice congee with crushed walnuts

Nourishing and slightly warming, warms the middle, builds up Qi, warms the stomach and spleen, harmonizes the intestine, forces Qi, reduces moisture.
Cooking time approx. 2 hours and more
Calories p. portion: 406
2 portions
Allergens: H

### Quantity of ingredients:
Basic recipe for a rice soup (Congee) 4 cups / 500g. (rec.) - neutral - sweet... *
Sugar cane sugar 2 table spoons / 20g. (little) - cool - sweet.....................earth
Walnuts 1 cup / 70g. (rec.) - warm - sweet..................................................earth
Cinnamon ground 1 pinch / 0,2g. (rec.) - hot - acrid, sweet.............................. *

### Cooking instructions:
Cook the basic recipe for rice soup (congee)
Note: The crushed walnuts can be cooked from the beginning.
Variation: Refine with sweet or spicy ingredients as you like. In particular, cinnamon, cloves, and ginger increase the warming effect and wholesomeness.

## 9.25 Rice dulse soup

Strengthens spleen and liver, regulates Qi flow, relaxes, builds up Qi, spreads, dries out, passes downwardly, strengthens stomach Qi, warms the stomach and spleen, harmonizes the intestine, forces Qi, reduces moisture.
Cooking time approx. 5 min
Calories p. portion: 190
2 portions
Allergens: L

### Quantity of ingredients:
Basic recipe for a rice soup (Congee) 4 cups / 500g. (rec.) - neutral - sweet... *
Basic recipe for a vegetable soup (nutritious) 2 cup / 500g. (rec.) - neutral - *. *
Dulse (seaweed) 2 table spoons / 15g. () - neutral - salty .........................water

### Cooking instructions:
Worm up a portion of pre-cooked basic recipe for a ricesoup (congee) and a portion pre-cooked basic recipe for a vegetable soup.
Bake the dulse in the oven at 220 degrees for 3 minutes. Spread the crisp dulse over the rice.

## 9.26 Rice noodle soup with shiitake mushrooms

Strengthens spleen and liver, regulates Qi flow, relaxes, builds up Qi, spreads, dries out, passes downwardly, strengthens stomach Qi, nourishes Yin of the lungs, stomach and colon, supports digestion.
Cooking time approx. 20 min
Calories p. portion: 66
2 portions
Allergens: L

### Quantity of ingredients:
Rice noodles 2 handful / 20g. (yes) - neutral - sweet ................................ metal
Shiitake, dried 4-6 pieces / 5g. (little) - neutral - sweet .............................. earth
Basic recipe for a vegetable soup (nutr.) 1 1/2 cups / 240g. (rec.) - neutral - * *
Chinese cabbage 1 cup / 60g. (yes) - cool - sweet ................................... earth
Lovage 1 teaspoon / 3g. (rec.) - warm - acrid, bitter ................................ metal
Miso 2 table spoons / 18g. (yes) - neutral - salty ...................................... water

### Cooking instructions:
Soak rice noodles and shiitake mushrooms separately in cold water. Heat the vegetable broth and add the soaked shiitake mushrooms cut into strips and simmer gently. Cut Chinese cabbage into noodles, add lovage green and rice noodles and let it steep for a while. Before serving, stir in Miso dissolved in a little cooled water.
Recommendation: Suitable at the beginning of each meal, also for breakfast

## 9.27 Rice with stewed vegetables

Dissipates heat and moisture.
Cooking time approx. 20 min
Calories p. portion: 166
2 portions
Allergens: L

### Quantity of ingredients:
Rice variety any 1/2 cup / 60g. (rec.) - warm - sweet ................................ metal
Water 3 cups / 300g. (yes) - cool - salty .................................................... earth
Lemon peel 1 piece / 3g. (rec.) - cool - bitter .............................................. fire
Water 1/2 cup / 0g. (yes) - cool - salty ....................................................... earth
Carrot 2 pieces / 180g. (rec.) - neutral - sweet .......................................... earth
Celery sticks 1/2 piece / 5g. (little) - cool - sweet ..................................... earth
Champignon 1/2 cup / 50g. (little) - cool - sweet ....................................... earth
Cress 2 table spoons / 20g. (little) - cool - sweet ...................................... metal
Linseed oil 1 dash / 3g. (little) - neutral - sweet ........................................ earth

**Cooking instructions:**
Cook rice according to basic recipe with a piece of lemon peel.
Steam chopped carrots, celery and mushrooms until soft.
Then sprinkle with cress. Then add a dash of high quality cold oil.

## 9.28 Sliced lamb with rosemary potatoes

Strengthens spleen and kidney Yang and stomach Qi, relieves
weakness, heats middle and lower heater, forces
Qi, relieves inflammation, moisturizes, relaxes, builds up Qi, spreads.
Cooking time approx. 1 hour
Calories p. portion: 461
4 portions
Allergens: LO

**Quantity of ingredients:**
Lamb meat 7/8 lbs - 1 lbs / 500g. (yes) - warm - sweet.................................fire
Olive oil 2 table spoons / 20g. (little) - cool - sweet ....................................earth
Onion white 1 piece / 50g. (yes) - warm - acrid.........................................metal
Garlic 1 clove / 2g. (little) - hot - acrid....................................................metal
Nutmeg 1 pinch / 0,2g. (rec.) - warm - acrid..............................................metal
Carrot 3 pieces / 150g. (rec.) - neutral - sweet..........................................earth
Celery root 1/4 tuber / 120g. (rec.) - cool - sweet .....................................earth
Rosemary 1 Twig / 3g. (rec.) - warm - bitter...............................................fire
Savory 1 teaspoon / 2g. (rec.) - warm - bitter............................................water
Parsley 1 table spoon / 8g. (rec.) - warm - bitter .......................................wood
Pepper powder (hot) 1 pinch / 2g. () - warm - bitter......................................fire
Red wine 1/2 cup / 125g. (yes) - warm - bitter.............................................fire
Lemon juice 1/2 piece / 15g. (rec.) - cold - sour .......................................wood
Cranberry 1 table spoon / 10g. (little) - cool - sour ....................................wood
Potato 6 pieces / 400g. (yes) - neutral - sweet...........................................earth

**Cooking instructions:**
Cut the lamb into strips, cut the carrots and celery into small cubes.
Heat the olive oil in a pan, fry the lamb in it, add the cut onions and
garlic, salt with herbal salt, a little water, parsley, deglaze with red wine,
season with paprika and small cut rosemary, mugwort, savory, carrots
and celery, turn the heat back on small Simmer for about 35 minutes.
Season with pepper and nutmeg, if necessary still salt, add a little
lemon juice, season with paprika, cranberries.
Cut the potatoes in half, the length of, spread a little olive oil on the cut
surface, salt, sprinkle 2-3 rosemary needles on each half potato, place
the potatoes on the baking sheet and bake in a preheated oven for
approx. 25 minutes at 190°C/374°F.

## 9.29 Tea from cinnamon sticks

Warms the stomach and spleen, promotes blood circulation and conduction flow, relieves cold-sickness and pain.
Cooking time approx. 15 min
Calories p. portion: 2
1 portion

**Quantity of ingredients:**
Cinnamon sticks 1/4 piece / 1g. (rec.) - hot - acrid, sweet................................ *
Water 1 cup / 125g. (yes) - cool - salty.....................................................earth

**Cooking instructions:**
A quarter of a cinnamon stick for a cup of tea. Start cold and bring to the boil. Let it sit for 15 minutes, then strain.
This tea is unsweetened and swallowed, slowly drunk. The amount is enough for one day.


## 9.30 Tea from juniper berry

Dries out, passes downwardly, activates Wei Qi.
Cooking time approx. 10 min
Calories p. portion: 10
1 portion

**Quantity of ingredients:**
Juniper berry 1 teaspoon / 3g. (rec.) - warm - sweet, acrid, bitter ................fire
Water 1 cup / 125g. (yes) - cool - salty.....................................................earth

**Cooking instructions:**
A teaspoon of dried juniper berries for a cup of tea. Start cold and bring to the boil. Let it sit for 15 minutes, then strain.
This tea is unsweetened and swallowed, slowly drunk. The amount is enough for one day.


## 9.31 Tea from raspberry leaves

Strengthens spleen Qi.
Cooking time approx. 10 min
Calories p. portion: 0
1 portion

**Quantity of ingredients:**
Water 1 cup / 250g. (yes) - cool - salty......................................................earth
Raspberry leaves 3 table spoons / 6g. (yes) ..................................................... *

**Cooking instructions:**
Heat the water till it boils and put it aside. Add raspberry leaves and leave for 10 min. to let go. Sweet to taste with honey. Strain when pouring.

## 9.32 Tea from thyme

Converts mucus, forces lungs and spleen, dries out, passes downwardly.
Cooking time approx. 10 min
Calories p. portion: 0
4 portions

**Quantity of ingredients:**
Thyme 3 table spoons / 6g. (rec.) - warm - bitter............................................... *
Water 2 cup water / 500g. (yes) - cool - salty ..............................................earth

**Cooking instructions:**
Heat the water till it boils and put it aside. Add thyme and 10 min. to let go. Strain. Sweet to taste with honey.
Drink 2 to 3 cups daily by mouth

## 9.33 Warming porridge

Forces Qi and defensive power.
Cooking time approx. 10 min
Calories p. portion: 357
1 portion
Allergens: AHO

**Quantity of ingredients:**
Oat flakes (whole grain) 6 table spoons / 60g. (rec.) - warm - sweet ........metal
Fig dried 3 pieces / 15g. (yes) - warm - sweet...........................................earth
Star anise 1 piece / 1g. (rec.) - hot - acrid .................................................metal
Ginger fresh 1 pinch / 0,5g. (rec.) - warm - acrid......................................metal
Water 1 cup / 120g. (yes) - cool - salty.......................................................earth
Maple syrup 1 table spoon / 10g. (yes) - cool - sweet ...............................earth
Walnuts 1 table spoon (chopped) / 8g. (rec.) - warm - sweet.....................earth

**Cooking instructions:**
Soak the dried fruit. Roast Oatmeal dry. Add dried ginger, star anise or cinnamon, a little grated ginger and boil everything with water to a mash. With maple syrup sweet. Whip grated walnuts and sprinkle before serving.

Effect: Suitable for the cold season.
Caution: Fresh ginger does not drink over a long period of time.

# 10 Effects of food

## 10.1 Use ingredients: recommendable

Anise (Common Fennel)
Apricot dried
Basic recipe for a chicken soup (warming)
Basic recipe for a fish soup
Basic recipe for a rice soup (Congee)
Basic recipe for a vegetable soup (nutritious)
Basil
Basil (fresh)
Beef fillet
Beef meat
Beef meat (calf)
Black caraway
Blueberry
Boxhorn clover seeds
Carp
Carrot
Carrot (Early Carrot)
Carrot juice without sugar
Celery root
Cereal coffee
Chestnuts
Chicken meat
Chili (pod or ground)
Chives
Cinnamon ground
Cinnamon sticks
Clove
Cocoa
Coriander
Corn Grease (Polenta)
Cumin (Caraway seed)
Dates dried
Dill
Fennel
Fish pieces mixed (fresh water)

Freshwater fish
Ginger fresh
Grass carp
Ground
Ground caraway
Hazelnuts
Hyssop
Juniper berry
Kohlrabi
Lemon juice
Lemon peel
Lovage
Marjoram
Mustard seeds
Nutmeg
Oat flakes (whole grain)
Oat flour
Oat fusion (baby food)
Oat meal
Oregano dried
Parsley
Parsley root
Parsnip
Pepper Cayenne
Pepper white (ground)
Peppercorns
Peppers (rose peppers)
Perch
Pine nuts
Plums
Pomegranate
Pumpkin seeds
Raisins
Raspberry leaf tea
Rice (whole grain)
Rice flour
Rice round grain

Rice sweet
Rice variety any
Rosemary
Salmon
Savory
Spelled (Dark) bread
Spelled semolina
Spelled wholemeal flour
Star anise
Sunflower seeds

Tarragon (Estragon)
Thyme
Trout
Tuna
Turkey breast meat
Vanilla
Vanilla powder
Walnuts
Water hot

## 10.2 Use ingredients: yes

Almond marzipan
Almond milk
Almond puree
Anchovy / Sardine
Apple (sweet)
Apricot
Apricots
Arrowroot
Asparagus (green or white)
Aubergine
Basic recipe for a beef soup (warming)
Beef bone marrow
Beef heart
Beef kidney
Beef liver
Beef lungs (calf)
Beef meatbones
Beef stomach
Bitter melon
Blackberry´s
Breadcrumbs (wheat bread, bread roll)
Broccoli
Brussels sprouts
Calamari
Cashews
Cauliflower
Cherry
Chicken egg
Chicken heart
Chicken liver
Chicken stomach
Chinese cabbage
Coconut flakes
Coconut grated
Coconut milk
Cod
Coriander (fresh)
Corn
Couscous
Crucian
Curry

Curry paste red
Eel
Fennel seeds ground
Fennel tea
Feta cheese
Fig
Fig dried
Goose
Goose egg
Goose parts
Gourd
Grape juice red
Grape juice white
Grapes red
Grapes white
Green spelt
Hawthorn
Herbs different varieties
Herbs of Provence
Herbs various
Herbs wild
Herring
Kumquats
Lamb bones
Lamb kidneys
Lamb liver
Lamb meat
Lamb shoulder
Leek
Lobster
Longane
Lychee
Lychee in Preserved
Malt
Maple syrup
Miso
Morel (black, dried)
Multi-grain bread (gray bread)
Octopus
Okra
Olives

Onion (shallot)
Onion (spring onion)
Onion read
Onion white
Oysters
Peaches
Peaches (canned)
Peanuts
Pear
Peas, green
Peppers
Pheasant
Pigeon
Pistachios
Plaice
Poppy
Potato
Pumpkin
Quail
Quail egg
Quinoa
Radish (white, green, purple-red)
Radish black
Radish horseradish
Radish leaves
Raspberry
Red cabbage
Red wine
Rice (fragrance)
Rice Basmati

Rice black
Rice long grain rice
Rice malt
Rice noodles
Rice red
Rice wild (nature rice)
Rose hip tea
Rye
Rye flour
Saffron
Sago (cereals)
Salsify
Shark
Shrimp
Soy Tofu
Soybean milk
Soybeans, black
Soybeans, yellow
Spelled flakes
Spelled grain
Spinach
Spiny lobsters
Sugar molasses
Sweet potato
Turmeric (yellow root)
Water
White bread (wheat bread)
White wine
Zucchini

## 10.3 Use ingredients: little

Adzuki beans
Apple (sour)
Artichoke
Balm
Bamboo shoots
Barley
Barley not peeled
Batavia
Bean oil
Berry juice
Black beans
Black-eyed peas
Blueberry juice
Boletus mushroom
Borage oil
Broad beans (thick beans)
Buckwheat
Buckwheat (roasted) Kasha
Bulgur (cereals)
Bush beans

Butter beans white
Celery sticks
Champignon
Chanterelle
Cherry juice
Chickpeas
Chicory
Chocolate
Clementines
Coffee
Coix (seeds) YiYi Ren
Cooking oil
Cow's milk (1.5% fat)
Cow's milk (whole milk 3.5% fat)
Cranberry
Cranberry juice
Cress
Currant (black)
Currant (red)
Currant (white)

Duck (heart)
Duck (slaughtered)
Elderberry blossom tee
Endive salad
Evening primrose oil
Fish remains
French beans
Fresh cheese
Garlic
Ginger oil
Ginger powder
Goat
Goat and sheep's milk
Goat cheese
Gooseberry
Grapefruit (Pomelo)
Grapefruit juice
Honey
Iceberg lettuce
Kidney beans (red)
Lamb's lettuce
Leaf salads (bitter)
Lentils
Lentils black
Lentils red
Lentils yellow
Lettuce
Lima beans
Linseed oil
Mackerel
Mallow (Malva sylvestris) blossom tea
Margarine
Margarine (diet)
Miso paste (soy bean paste)
Mold cheese
Morel, dried
Mozzarella
Mung bean
Mung bean sprouting
Mutton
Mutton
Olive oil
Oyster mushroom
Parmesan
Peanut oil
Pear juice
Peas
Pimento
Pinto beans speckled
Pork heart
Pork kidneys
Pork knuckle
Pork liver

Pork meat
Pork skin
Pork stomach
Pumpkin seed oil
Quince
Rabbit
Rabbit liver
Rabbit meat
Radicchio
Radish
Rapeseed oil
Raspberry dried (immature)
Reishi mushroom
Romaine lettuce / lettuce salad
Rosefish
Sage
Salt
Sauerkraut (cutted cabbage fermented)
Sesame oil
Shiitake, dried
Sour cherries
Soy sauce
Soybean oil
Spirit
Strawberries
Strawberry Juice
Sugar brown
Sugar candy white
Sugar cane sugar
Sugar fructose - fruit sugar
Sugar glucose - grapes sugar
Sugar Milk Sugar
Sugar white
Sunflower oil
Tangerine
Thistle oil
Tsampa (roasted barley flour)
Umeboshi plums (Japanese apricots)
Vegetable juice
Vinegar (Apple vinegar)
Vinegar (Red wine vinegar)
Vinegar Aceto Balsamico
Walnut oil
Wheat germ oil
White beans
Wild boar meat
Wormwood

## 10.4 Do not use contra-acting foods

Agar agar (kelp)
Amaranth
Avocado
Banana
Banana (cooking banana)
Basic recipe for a duck soup
Beer (Pils)
Beer (Top-fermented German dark beer)
Black tea
Burdock root tea
Butter organic
Buttermilk
Cantaloupe
Carambola (Star fruit)
Caviar
Chard
Chlorella (fresh water)
Crab
Cream, sweet 30%
Crème fraiche cheese
Cucumber
Curd cheese 20%
Curd cheese 40%
Dandelion (young plants)
Dandelionroots tea
Deer meat
Deer meat
Green tea
Kefir
Kiwi
Kombu seaweed (Saccharina japonica)
Lady's mantle
Lemon
Lime
Mango
mango powder
Mediterranean fish (cod, plaice, haddock, sea Millet

Millet flakes
Mineral water
Mulberry fruit
Mullet
Mussels
Oat
Oat flakes roasted
Orange
Orange juice
Papaya
Pineapple
Pineapple (from a can)
Pineapple juice without sugar
Plum
Rhubarb
Sake
Seacrab
Sorrel
Sour cream (Schmand) 30% fat
Sour cream 15% fat
Sour milk
Sour milk cheese 20%
Tomato
Wakame
Watermelon
Wheat
Wheat beer
Wheat bran
Wheat bulgur
Wheat flakes
Wheat flour
Wheat semolina
Wheat semolina for children
Wheatgrass powder
Yarrow tea
Yogi tea
Yogurt (natural, 1.5% fat)
Yogurt (natural, 3.5% fat)

# 11 Complementary

## 11.1 Agrimony

Agrimonia eupatoria
preparation: Healing tea (infusion)
Moves and regulates Liver-Qi and Gallbladder-Qi, astringent, quenches

bleeding, strengthens Spleen-Qi and Stomach-Qi, transforms moisture, dissipates Moisture-Heat.
The herb contains many bitter and tannins and therefore helps as a tea in gastrointestinal diseases and liver disease. As a gargle, however, also relieves gingivitis, sore throat and coughing.
Dosage: 1-4 g of dried tea as a decoction, 1-4 ml tincture

## 11.2 Buckeye

Aesculus hippocastanum, fol.
preparation: Different effects
Moves blood, strengthens the middle, Supports the spleen while holding the blood and lifting the qi. Astringent. Moves Liver-Qi, Moves Liquids.
Active ingredients: Aesculus saponins, tannins, flvonglycosides
Dosage: Note: Nit use in pregnancy, sensitive stomach.

## 11.3 Caraway

Carum carvi
preparation: Healing tea (infusion)
Warms spleen qi and stomach-qi, strengthens yang spleen, kidney and heart. Moves lung-qi.

# 12 Basics of Nutrition

The basic principles of nutrition described herein are general recommendations. They are not aimed at a specific form of therapy. Recommendations concerning a therapy have priority.

## 12.1 Nutrition

Regular meals in a relaxed atmosphere. A warm breakfast is considered a good start into the day.

The main meals ought to be taken for lunch – supper in the early evening. Pay attention to feeling hungry or sated: don't eat too much nor remain hungry is the rule

Prepare the meals freshly from natural, regional products. Frozen, heat-conserved, industrially prepared or foodstuffs cooked in the microwave oven are rejected.

Choice of foodstuffs according to the season: more cooling food in summer, more warming food in winter.

Eat cooked food at least twice a day. Food and drinks ought to be lukewarm, never ice-cold or hot.

Raw vegetables, briefly cooked vegetables, freshly squeezed juices and mineral water are not recommended. Milk and dairy products are only included in the diet if they don't cause problems.

Don't use therapeutic recipes over a longer period without consulting your doctor or therapist.

### Varied food
Enjoy the diversity of foodstuffs. Characteristics of a balanced nutrition are variety, suitable combination and a balanced quantity of rich and low energy foodstuffs (on one hand avoiding undersupply with essential nutrients and on the other hand to take to many undesirable substances).

### A lot of Cereal Products - and Potatoes
Bread, pasta, rice, cereal flakes (best wholemeal) as well as potatoes contain almost no fat, but many vitamins, mineral nutrients, trace elements, roughage and secondary plant substances. These foodstuffs ought to be taken with low-fat side dishes.

### Vegetables and Fruit – „Take Five" every day ...
5 portions of vegetables and fruit a day, as fresh as possible, briefly cooked, or maybe one portion as a juice – ideal as a side dish to every meal as well as snack between meals: Thus a lot of vitamins, mineral nutrients as well as roughage and secondary plant substances

**Daily milk and dairy products**
Milk and Dairy Products every Day, once or twice per Week Fish;
meat, sausages as well as eggs moderately. These foodstuffs contain
valuable nutrients like calcium in the milk, iodine selenium and omega-3
fat acids in saltwater fish. Meat is favorable due to its high content of
disposable iron and the vitamins B1, B6 and B12. Quantities of 300 – 600
g meat and sausage per week are sufficient. Prefer low-fat products,
especially in meat- and dairy products.

**Low-fat and fatty Foodstuffs**
Fat supplies us with essential fat acids and fatty foodstuffs contain also
fat-soluble vitamins. Fat is high in energy; therefore much fat in the food
may cause overweight, possibly also cancer. Too many saturated fat
acids may further a tendency for cardio-vascular diseases in the long
term. Prefer vegetable oils and fats (e.g. rapeseed-, olive-, soya-oils and
solid fats produced therefrom). Beware of invisible fat in meat- and dairy
products, pastry and sweets as well as in fast-food and convenience
foods. 70 – 90 g fat per day is sufficient.

**Moderately Sugar and Salt**
Take sugar and foods/drinks containing various kinds of sugar (e.g.
glucose syrup) only occasionally. Use herbs and spices as well as a little
salt creatively. Prefer salt containing iodine.

**Plenty of Liquids**
Water is absolutely essential. Drink 1-2 l liquids every day. Prefer water
(with or without gas) and other low-calorie drinks. Alcoholic drinks should
not be taken.

**Tasty Dishes, carefully cooked**
Cook the meals with as low temperatures and as short as possible, using
little water and fat – this preserves the original taste, keeps the nutrients
intact and prevents the production of harmful compounds.

**Take time and enjoy the food**
Take your Time and enjoy your Food
Eating consciously helps to eat right. The eye enjoys food, too. It's fun,
invites to enjoy varied dishes and stimulates the feeling of satiety.

**Watch your Weight and stay in Motion**
A balanced diet and a lot of exercise and sport (30 – 60 min/day) are a
healthy combination. The right weight furthers well-being and health.
Thermals, directional effectiveness, digestive power

There are various criteria for judging the effectiveness of herbs and foodstuffs.

The use of certain herbs and ingredients is based on observations of the effects on the body which these foodstuffs, herbs and spices show after having eaten them. The medical science has developed following system: Every ingredient or herb has a directional effectiveness. Furthermore, there are herbs which have a special effect on certain organs.

The basic condition for a healthy metabolism is to obtain sufficient energy from food and that the digestive process doesn't use too much energy. An easily digestible meal makes content and sated, doesn't cause flatulence and fatigue after the meal. The perfect spices increase the healthiness of our meals. Very often, just small doses of herbs and spices will suffice. They are not used to make us sated, but to help our digestive organs to digest the food.

## 12.2 Recipes

The recipes list the ingredients to be used and the cooking instructions show how the dish is prepared. The list of ingredients shows the concerned quantities as well as the relevance for the therapy. If you find „less than mentioned", try to comply or find an alternative from the „list of recommended foodstuffs". Mostly it shall result just in a small change of taste when you simply avoid this ingredient.

Mild cooking methods: boiling, stewing, poaching, steaming
Strong cooking methods: barbecuing, roasting, frying, smoking
Balanced cooking methods: deep-frying, baking brick
Deep-freezing and warming in the microwave oven should be avoided (denaturalization).

## 12.3 Foodstuffs

Foodstuffs have an effect on body and soul like medicinal herbs, only a very much milder one. Dietary advice is mainly based on regional foodstuffs. The knowledge about the effects of each foodstuff and the knowledge, when which foodstuff shall be used, is based on the orthodox school of medicine. Use ecologic-organic products, if possible. As everything should be cooked for a long time due to a better digestability and very rarely eaten raw, the food agrees with everyone.

The classification of the foodstuffs according to their effect on the body is the basis in order to achieve a harmonious status of health.

Dietary advisors do not recommend certain foodstuffs for everyone. The individual diet is tailor-made for the individual constitution.

Buy only fresh and ripe fruit and vegetables. You ought to leave unripe fruit and vegetables and such with brown spots and wilted leaves behind in the market. In this case take deep-frozen goods (never ready-to-serve dishes!). Fruit and vegetables are deep-frozen immediately after harvesting and often contain more vitamins and minerals than the goods from the vegetable shelf. Whereas conserved or tinned goods contain very much less biological substances. Also, salt, sugar and others are mostly added to the latter. Never leave the foodstuffs in the water after washing them to avoid that many vital substances get drowned. Clean salads, fruit and vegetables immediately before serving.

Please make sure of the hygienic processing of foodstuffs. Clean your salads, fruit and vegetables carefully. When cooking with meat, prepare all ingredients first and then process the meat products. Clean the worktop and tools very carefully. Wooden surfaces ought to be treated with a mild disinfectant regularly in order to reduce germination.

Store fruit and vegetables separately, if possible. Harvested fruit and vegetables are still alive and emit e.g. ethylene gas, which makes other products ripen and age faster. Keep meat and fish in the closed packaging or store them in the fridge in closed containers.

## 12.4 Herbs

There are some basic rules for storing medicinal herbs. On principle, herbs must be protected from direct sunlight, humidity and heat.

Containers for the storage of herbs may be glasses, ceramic jars and even plastic containers. However, plastic is a rather unsuitable material and should only be a short-term solution. In case of glass containers, use a dark material.

Medicinal herbs cannot be kept for any long period. The shelf life of herbs is limited. However, it can be prolonged with suitable storage. The place should be dark, rather cool and absolutely dry. A wooden medicine cabinet, placed not directly next to a source of heat, would be ideal. Never buy large quantities of herbs so as not to have to throw them away. Label the container with the name of the herb and the date of harvesting or processing.

# 13 Other dietic-books

The following syndromes of dietetics, TCM or for a therapy supplement for cancer are available.

## Dietetics

E001. Nutrition of the infant - baby food
E002. Nutrition during lactation
E003. Nutrition in old age
E004. Nutrition of children and adolescents
E005. Nutrition of athletes
E006. Light weight
E007. Pregnancy
E008. Full food

**Protein and electrolyte - kidneys**
E009. (hemodialysis) dialysis treatment
E010. Acute renal failure
E011. Chronic renal insufficiency
E012. Nephrotic syndrome
E013. Kidney stones (nephrolithiasis)

**Gastrointestinal tract - pancreas**
E014. Acute pancreatitis (inflammation of the pancreas)
E015. Chronic pancreatitis (inflammation of the pancreas)

**Gastrointestinal tract - small intestine and large intestine**
E016. Acute obstipation (constipation)
E017. Chronic obstipation (constipation)
E018. Colon irritabile
E019. Diverticulitis
E020. Acquired lactose intolerance (lactose malabsorption)
E021. Fructose malabsorption
E022. Glutensensitive enteropathy (celiac disease)
E023. Colectomy
E024. Short Bowel Syndrome

**Gastrointestinal tract - liver, gallbladder, bile ducts**
E025. Acute and chronic hepatitis (inflammation of the liver)
E026. Cholelithiasis (bile stones)
E027. fatty liver
E028. cirrhosis

**Gastrointestinal tract - Stomach and duodenal intestine**
E029. Acute gastritis
E030. Chronic gastritis
E031. Stomach bleeding
E032. Ulcus ventriculi and duodenal ulcer
E033. Condition after gastric surgery

### Gastrointestinal tract - oral cavity and esophagus
E034. Stomatitis
E035. Esophageal carcinoma (esophageal cancer)
E036. Refluosophagitis (heartburn)

### Special diseases
E037. Phenylketonuria (PKU)
E038. Rheumatic joint diseases

### Metabolism
E039. Obesity (overweight)
E040. Diabetes mellitus
E041. Eating disorders (underweight)

### Fat metabolism
E042. Hypercholesterolaemia (increased cholesterol level)
E043. Hepatic Encephalopathy

### Heart and circulation
E044. Arteriosclerosis (arterial calcification)
E045. Heart insufficiency
E046. Hypertension
E047. Hyperuricaemia and gout

### Changed nutrient requirements
E048. In case of fever
E049. For malignant diseases
E050. After burns
E051. Radiation and chemotherapy

## CANCER
E100. Pancreatic cancer
E101. Bladder cancer
E102. Blood cancer (leukemia)
E103. Breast cancer
E104. Colorectal cancer
E105. Gastric cancer
E106. Kidney cancer
E107. Esophageal cancer

## TCM
E200. Bladder - moisture heat in the bladder
E201. Bladder - moisture and cold in the bladder
E202. Bladder - emptiness and cold in the bladder
E203. Large intestine - external cold affects the large intestine
E204. Large intestine - moisture heat in the large intestine
E205. Large intestine - heat blocks the intestine II acute
E206. Large intestine - dryness of the colon
E207. Large intestine - Yang deficiency (cold)
E208. Heart - Blood insufficiency
E209. Heart - Blood stagnation
E210. Heart - Fire
E211. Heart - Hot mucus clogs the heart pores

E212. Heart - Cold mucus clogs the heart pores
E213. Heart - Qi deficiency
E214. Heart - Yang deficiency
E215. Heart - Yin deficiency
E216. Liver - Ascending Liver Yang
E217. Liver - Blood deficiency
E218. Liver - Blood stagnation
E219. Liver - Moisture heat in liver and gall bladder
E220. Liver - Fire
E221. Liver - Gall bladder Qi-Empty
E222. Liver - Cold in the liver meridian
E223. Liver - Qi stagnation
E224. Liver - Wind
E225. Liver - Wind with ascending liver Yang
E226. Liver - Wind with blood anemic
E227. Liver - Wind with extreme heat
E228. Lung - Qi deficiency
E229. Lung - Mucus-moisture in the lungs
E230. Lung - Mucus-heat in the lungs
E231. Lung - Mucus-cold in the lungs
E232. Lung - Dryness of the lungs
E233. Lung - Wind-heat attacks the lungs
E234. Lung - Wind-cold affects the lungs
E235. Lung - Yin deficiency
E236. Stomach - Bloodstagnation
E237. Stomach - Fire
E238. Stomach - Cold with liquid
E239. Stomach - Nutrition stagnation
E240. Stomach - Qi deficiency
E241. Stomach - Rebellious Qi
E242. Stomach - Yin Emptiness
E243. Spleen - Heat and moisture attack the spleen
E244. Spleen - Coldness and moisture affects the spleen
E245. Spleen - Qi deficiency
E246. Spleen - Qi deficiency + Declining spleen Qi
E247. Spleen - Qi deficiency + spleen does not control the blood
E248. Spleen - Yang deficiency
E249. Kidney - Heart and kidney no longer communicate
E250. Kidney - Jing deficiency
E251. Kidney - Kidneys cannot receive the Qi
E252. Kidney - Qi is not stable
E253. Kidney - Yang deficiency
E254. Kidney - Yin deficiency


For further information visit di-book.com.


# 14 EBNS - Software for nutritional counseling

The main task of the database is to create personalized nutritional advice
for each patient individually. The database was developed for Dietetics

and Traditional Chinese Medicine.
The Database supports training and advices in the daily work routine.

The computer program provides lists of recipes, ingredients and herbs, which are given to the client. individually adjustable according to patient's request from whole food to vegetarians (lacto, ovo, ...). For every register there is an information sheet which can be given to the client. All texts can be individually designed.

The syndromes can be combined and result in an intersection of the recommended recipes and ingredients. The automated diagnosis for the TCM enables you to check your experience during the training as well as to confirm your diagnosis in the working day. You select several predefined symptoms and have the program automatically display the relevant syndromes.

How to work with the database:
Select the patient / client, select one or more of the syndromes you diagnosed and print the folder.

You can change all values, create new symptoms or syndromes, develop recipes, change or adapt ingredients and herbs to your findings. In simple client management, all relevant data about the person is stored. You get an overview of the past diagnoses and the development of the course of the disease.

As a consultant you save a lot of time when you print out the recipe, food and herbal lists for the recognized syndromes and give them to the clients. You can use this time for a personal conversation. With the database, dieticians and nutritionists can view the nutrients and trace elements for each recipe and develop recipes for syndromes even with suggested ingredients.

All recipe and grocery lists can also be ordered from me as a combination of several diseases. I wish all readers good luck, health and happiness in life.
More information can be found at www.ebns.at.
Volunteer: www.krebsinfo.at
Josef Miligui